The Ministry of Cheerfulness

by
Jesse Duplantis

JESSE DUPLANTIS MINISTRIES
"Preaching the Gospel to the World"

The Ministry of Cheerfulness
ISBN 978-0-9728712-0-4
Copyright © 1993 by Jesse Duplantis
All Rights Reserved. Published 1993

9th Printing 2009
Published by Jesse Duplantis Ministries
PO Box 1089
Destrehan, Louisiana 70047 USA
www.jdm.org

Jesse Duplantis Ministries is dedicated to reaching people and changing lives with the Gospel of Jesus Christ. For more information, or to purchase other products from Jesse Duplantis Ministries, please contact us at the address above.

Contents

Chapter One

The Ministry of Cheerfulness

Cheerfulness is infectious! I love to spread the joy of the Lord everywhere I go. No matter where I am, or what I'm doing, I make it a point to infect others with good cheer.

Of course, I wasn't always this way. I've had to learn through the Word just how to keep the joy of the Lord flowing in my life. I pray that as you read, you will be challenged to incorporate the joy of the Lord in your own life. It is the only way to go!

I guarantee you that if you'll listen to and stick with the things of God, you will live an overcoming life.

You will infect everyone around you with the precious, healing joy of the Lord. Your ministry can and will be one of cheerfulness.

I acquired a pencil sketch of Jesus, laughing and full of joy, years ago while ministering during a session at a well-known Bible school. A student, whom I know only as Suzanne, blessed my wife and me with a drawing of what she described as "the Jesus you preach about. " As she gave it, she told us that after hearing me minister she was inspired to draw Him in a different way, full of joy and laughter.

To her, I shared a side of Jesus that she had never heard about. I had to admit after seeing the picture that, although I knew Jesus to be the author of my joy, I had never seen a picture of Him laughing.

My wife and I loved it so much that we had it framed and hung it in our foyer. We wanted the joyful face of Jesus to be the very first thing that visitors to our home would see.

Now, that picture has gotten mixed reactions. Some people can never picture Jesus in a cheerful way. His eyes shining with love and squinting from laughter are just too much for them to handle. They think that Jesus lived every moment of His life solemn and serious.

But I believe that He had many joyful times in His life here on earth. If He hadn't, the children would have never come to Him so readily while they were playing. They were laughing and probably tumbling all over the grass, just horseplaying like kids do. I imagine Jesus was smiling ear to ear as He watched them play. I believe it was His joy that put those kids at ease and caused them all to want to be near Him.

Both adults and children alike were drawn to Jesus because He was a man with a ministry of cheerfulness.

Jesus ministered joy, peace and hope while He was here on earth, and He continues to do it today through His Spirit and His Word.

In John 16:33, Jesus told His disciples: *These things I have spoken unto you, that in me ye might have peace. In the world ye shall have tribulation: but be of good cheer; I have overcome the world.*

I'm always amazed at how many Christians are shocked when trouble surfaces in their lives. Although Jesus warned us that it would happen, they have this idea that salvation through Christ brings a candy-coated life. Jesus plainly said that while we were in the world we would have tribulation or trouble. But He commanded us to be of good cheer, because He's overcome this world.

So when trouble comes, don't be shocked! Be of good cheer, be reminded that Jesus has overcome this world and every circumstance in it!

The devil is just stupid enough to make the Word of God come to pass. The boy doesn't have a lick of sense! You'd think that he'd leave us all alone just to try to prove the Word wrong. But, of course, he's too stupid to come up with any bright ideas.

When the devil sends trouble your way, don't buckle under his attack by singing, "Gloom, despair and agony on me! Deep, dark depression, excessive misery!" No way! Refuse to agree with that idiot! Don't major on the tribulation, major on the fact that Jesus has overcome the world. He's won! And we've been made more than conquerors through His victory!

Do you know that even in times of tribulation, joy doesn't have to leave you? Jesus said it is possible to be in peace and of good cheer, even in the midst of tribulation, because He has overcome the world.

Really, it's totally up to you. You have a choice to either trust God or worry. You choose joy or you choose anxiety. Either way, you are going to be confronted with trouble in this life. Jesus said it would happen, so there is no changing that. But what you can change is whether you'll go through it in misery or overcome it in joy. I'll tell you from experience that I've tried both ways, and joy is definitely the way to go !

I heard someone say once the key to being successful doesn't depend on what you've been dealt in life, but how you "deal" with what is dealt. In other words, your reaction to the trouble is what is going to determine your success in this life.

Just because you've got some trouble doesn't mean you have to lose joy. You can make a choice to be full of cheer, because you know that Jesus has already overcome. It's your part to enforce Satan's defeat by rebuking him and standing on the Word.

When trouble comes in my life, I say to the devil, "You idiot! You've just proved the Word of God is true! And if this part is true, then it all is! So devil, get ready because I'm going to blast your plans for my defeat.

Jesus made me victorious through His blood, and it's in His name that I command you to take your hands off my life! Devil, I enjoy telling you that you are defeated and I have overcome! I laugh at your trouble and enjoy not giving you the pleasure of seeing me buckle under it! You fool, get under my feet! "

You see, I'd rather laugh at the trouble than align myself with it. If I give in to the trouble and begin rehearsing the problem, the joy of the Lord in my life is suddenly replaced with worry and anxiety. I've learned that in order to keep that joy, I must major on the promise and not the problem. Jesus has already overcome, and He's given all authority and power to me! Realizing and believing that is the key to not losing any of that precious joy.

Living in the joy of the Lord is one of the most effective ways to reach others for Christ.

Every human on the earth is searching for joy. It's the one thing everybody wants out of life. Joy opens doors that once were locked shut! If you choose to live in joy, others will be literally drawn to you. They won't know why, but they'll just love being around you! Some will even ask you why you are always so cheerful. Jesus will use your joy to draw others in so that you can share the Gospel with them. He wants to have a relationship with them so badly, He's going to use any and every avenue you allow Him to in order to reach them.

But if you choose to allow the devil and circumstances to replace your joy with anxiety, you will have a hard time reaching others for Christ through your witness. You'll have to almost chase people down just to tell them about God. And when you finally catch them, you'll have a hard time trying to convince them that what you have is worth having.

Think about it. Who would want to accept the God of someone who lives beaten down and depressed? I mean, if it ain't working for you, why should they believe that it will work for them? It's just a fact that people who are familiar with you will pay more attention to what you do and how you live, than what you say to them. So be cheerful!

Replace the moaning and groaning, criticizing and complaining with the promises God's given you in His Word. Quit looking at what the devil's done and start looking at what God's done! He's made you more than a conqueror! If He's for you, who can be against you? He's the Alpha and Omega, the beginning and the end. He's overcome this world and everything in it! He's living inside of you, friend!

So believe it and dig into His Word. Find every promise you can and dwell in that secret place of the Most High. Walk in His Spirit joyfully every day because He's got places for you to go and people for you to meet! His joy will make you like a magnet for the unsaved, broken-hearted. You won't have to go get them. They'll come get you!

But the joy of the Lord isn't just limited to being an effective witnessing tool. According to Proverbs 17:22, *A merry heart doeth good like a medicine; but a broken spirit drieth the bones.* Joy can keep you well like medicine! I read one time that most of the hospitals in this country are filled with people whose problems stem from stress, worry and anxiety.

Your body wasn't created to live worrying about every little thing! You were created to walk in the joy of the Lord every day of your life. His joy can keep you living well!

I love living with the joy of the Lord in my soul! It's taken me out of the heart of the mullygrubs and into the heart of Glory! Now, I don't claim to be perfect. Just like you, I recognize the areas of my life that need to be renewed daily in the Word of God.

I've blamed my temper on my Cajun heritage for years. I've tried to justify it by telling God, "It's that Tabasco Sauce that Mama put in my baby bottle that makes me do this!" It's so easy to find a reason why. Justification for the flesh is so many believers' specialty. But we've all got to learn to get honest with God. It's not like He can't see through the wool we try to pull over His eyes.

The three main things I do when I mess up are:

1. Admit it.

2. Repent, ask for forgiveness and turn the other way.

3. Refuse to let the devil hold it over my head.

Number three is very important because you must remember that God forgives and forgets. He's not going to bring up what you did last week if you've already repented. Only the devil tries to condemn you with the past. When that idiot tries to remind you of anything God's forgiven you for, tell him to shut up! It's okay, God has given you the right to tell him where to go (i.e., hell). Just press your heel down a little tighter on his neck, and resist the thoughts of inadequacy he tries to put on you. God has forgiven you and wants you to get back up and start living in joy again. Refill yourself with joy by getting in the Word and dwelling in the secret place of the Most High.

On a daily basis I accept a portion of joy, the holy fire, and I confront problems with promises. If sickness tries to attach itself to my body, I confront it with 1 Peter 2:24, *Who his own self bare our sins in his own body on the tree, that we, being dead to sins, should live unto righteousness: by whose stripes ye were healed.*

In situations of financial difficulty, I enforce Philippians 4:19, *But my God shall supply all your need according to his riches in glory by Christ Jesus.*

If I begin to get weary, I go to the Word and get filled. I remember God's promise in 1 Corinthians 15:58, *Therefore, my beloved brethren, be ye stedfast, unmoveable, always abounding in the work of the Lord, forasmuch as ye know that your labour is not in vain in the Lord.* Jesus has overcome! He has a promise for every problem you've got. His promises are always bigger than the problems. The devil is really no match for God or His people!

Life can be very intense and fast paced. Those who run hard often faint, and those who cannot run are often in despair.

Life can be difficult if you are trying to live it on your own. The world is fast paced, and the "survival of the fittest" is the prevailing mentality. But, praise God, you and I don't have to live the way they do! We've been called to walk a different path than the rest of the world. He's given us a better route. If we'll run the race He's set before us with joy, it'll be much easier to avoid fainting along the way.

Today there are many believers running in the wrong race. Unknowingly they trot along, leaning on their own understanding and standing in their own strength. Although they want to believe the Bible and trust in God, they always seem to end up relying more on themselves and those around them rather than on Jesus. Consequently, their lives show it. They live pretty defeated and don't have much joy for themselves, much less anyone else.

There are a few different types of people who do this. Some people constantly speak about what the devil's done in their lives. They are always focusing on the problems of life and have a real hard time being cheerful. Because of so many past defeats, they've become people with no confidence in themselves or in God. They say they'll never do anything, and so they don't. The devil has convinced them that they are useless.

If you are like some of those who have no confidence in themselves, but you want the ministry of cheerfulness to become a reality in your life, there is a way to gain that joy. Renewing your hope in Jesus and renewing your mind through His Word are the keys to gaining confidence in yourself.

Go back and find out what Jesus did for you on the cross and what rights His blood bought for you. Research all that you have been made through Him. It'll stir you up ! It will cause you to begin focusing on Him instead of on the circumstances. Your mind has got to come off those problems and on to His promises. Hope needs to be nurtured.

Hope is earnest expectation that God will do what He said. Hope gets the pressure off you, and allows you to begin to stand on His Word and in His strength. When you begin to have hope, then faith can start to work. Faith is what gets those mountains to be thrown into the sea. But you can't have faith until you have some hope. So, get intimate with Jesus, read His Word and worship Him with a true heart! Drawing close to Him will build you up. As His Word becomes real to you, hope will come easily and then faith will too. When He is your focus, joy becomes inevitable! Choose to dwell on the fact that Jesus has already overcome!

Offices are not measured by their prominence, but by the fidelity in which they are carried out.

Another type of people who have trouble being cheerful are those who feel as if they never win the prizes in life. The high positions are always given to someone else. Somebody else always gets the job. They begin to complain about it, and self-pity starts to choke their joy. Consequently, they are discouraged by any job they are given that doesn't seem prominent enough.

If you feel this way, I must tell you that God's offices are not measured by prominence. They are measured by the fidelity in which they are filled. God doesn't overlook anything noble! What you consider small, He considers very important, and He rewards those things that you do with a good heart. No matter what it is, God wants you to be faithful with what He's placed in your hands. You have a job that you need to do with joy! It is important, and you need to know it!

Did you know that there are those in life that only you can reach for Jesus? It is true! God has purposes and plans for you, friend. Be faithful, God will reward your diligence!

A veteran is never useless, and spiritual service is not measured by physical strength.

Then there are those who have been running the race for many years. They ran on the right path faithfully and saw God do many extraordinary things through their lives. Joyfully they ran for many, many years. But time went on, and somewhere along the way they began to slow down. They were fainting, becoming weary in well doing. Eventually the devil convinced them that they were no longer needed. They began thinking of "retiring" instead of "refiring."

A veteran is never useless, and spiritual service is not measured by physical strength. It doesn't matter what your age in the faith, you can be a powerful force for the Gospel.

Did you know that Abraham did his best when he was one hundred years old? He considered not his own body and staggered not at the promise of God. It has nothing to do with how much power, intellect or how many qualifications you have. The only thing that matters is how faithful you are to the call of God. Faith in God will make you an overcomer and enable you to be effective no matter what your age in the faith.

While holding a revival meeting, the pastor invited me to speak at a luncheon for the widows in his church. These elderly women, most of them were in their 80s, were strong women of faith and had lived for God most of their lives. One of the women who sat next to me just sparkled with the fire of the Holy Ghost. I looked at her and said, "You have fire!"

She looked up at me and exclaimed, "I certainly do!"

When I jokingly asked her if she was planning on having another baby, she looked me right in the eye and said, "I'm not 90 yet!" She had learned to daily "refire" the gift of God in her life. The joy of the Lord had been her strength for some time and she wasn't even thinking about retiring in the faith.

Joy is going to be refired through relationship with Jesus. Trust in Him, and you will be free in this life. Free to be an overcomer, full of His joy. Man, it's easy to live smiling when you know God has it all under control! He can handle it all!

You can be an encourager to everyone you meet. When the joy of the Lord dominates you, true encouragement is unconscious. You'll encourage others without even realizing it! Let God flow through you to others. It's our purpose to have fellowship with Jesus and impart life and joy to others. We can be used to change lives! Joy, that holy fire, keeps our purpose warm and our intelligence aglow.

Cheerfulness is infectious, but stupidity is aggravating.

Did you ever meet people who had more stupidity than God-given joy? They are like a flash of lightning, lighting up the sky and breaking through the gloom for a moment. They are like happiness, dazzling brightly and then disappearing without a trace. Happiness is an emotion that is short-lived and can be reversed by the first signs of trouble.

Joy is not an emotion, it is a spiritual force that you live with, day in and day out. Your ministry of cheerfulness doesn't shut down just because tribulation comes. God-given joy stands throughout every attack of the enemy.

Cheerfulnesss is fixed and permanent. While in the Garden of Gethsemane, Jesus prayed, *Abba, Father, all things are possible unto thee; take away this cup from me: neverthelesss not what I will, but what thou wilt* (Mark 14:36). Problems and difficulty did not change Jesus, because He knew that He came into the world to defeat death for all mankind on the cross.

Cheerfulness comes from knowing the Good News. When the devil throws his fiery darts of gloom, you have a shield of faith against depression. Get your shield up! Happiness also can be produced by helping others. Considering your neighbor over yourself is the ladder out of misery and unhappiness. By helping others, you have the opportunity to see yourself in a different perspective. Meeting someone else's need requires you to break from self-consumption.

A few years ago, I was scheduled to minister in a rather large church. It was my first time there, and I was waiting with the pastor in his office before the evening service began. He kept huffing and puffing, sneaking out to see how the church was filling up, getting more and more irritated as the service time drew closer. I finally asked him what the problem was, and after telling me that the church was only half full, he exclaimed, "I just couldn't preach to this crowd! It's too small!"

I was shocked by his attitude, and I wondered how he ever managed to make the church grow to this size. I said, "You know what your problem is? You came to have the people meet your need, but you should have come to help meet their need. If you'll do that, it won't matter if two people show up or two million. "

You see, that pastor's priorities had gotten out of line. His cheerfulness had been robbed because he'd become totally consumed with himself. His main focus was not on the people or their needs, but on himself.

Just as Jesus does with us, He expects us to prefer others over ourselves. As you spend time developing an intimate relationship with Him, preferring others will become your heartbeat. Love for others will overtake you and a powerful ministry of cheerfulness will begin to grow within you !

As you daily run the race set before you, Jesus will ignite a holy fire in you that will fill you with joy overflowing! There's nothing like living for Him!

Chapter Two

Living Letters

Let's face it, the proof is in the pudding! The only Jesus some people will ever see is the Jesus in you or the Jesus in me. The only way they will understand His love is by seeing it in action through His Body.

The Apostle Paul said, *Ye are our epistle written in our hearts, known and read of all men:*

Forasmuch as ye are manifestly declared to be the epistle of Christ ministered by us, written not with ink, but with the Spirit of the living God; not in tables of stone, but in fleshy tables of the heart (2 Cor. 3:2,3).

What are epistles? They are not apostles' wives as some might think! They are letters or messages for the world to read! As Paul spoke of the Corinthians being epistles, we too are living letters.

A Living Letter is an unfinished life. The last page will not be written until the Kingdom and the will of God are done on the earth.

Every person who is born again can reveal a side of Jesus that the world has never seen. Every believer is made in His image, and all have uniqueness in Him. Our lives should be read like a page of large, clear print which will lead them to quick, calculating conclusions.

I have been in meetings where some people get boisterous while praising Jesus. Others, in the same meeting, barely move, yet seem to enjoy the service just as much. The loud one wonders why the quiet one isn't moving. He asks himself, "What's the matter with this guy? Is he dead?" No, he's not dead, he is just a side of God that you are not used to. When we are critical of other believers, we are critical of Jesus. He lives in them and has given them a uniqueness only they possess.

Luke said in Acts 1: 1, *The former treatise have I made, O Theophilus, of all that Jesus began both to do and teach.* In other words, the twelve disciples were going to show a side of Jesus that the world had never seen.

A human life is the medium in which God's voice utters divine truths. Jesus began the work when He was on earth and is still continuing through the Body of Christ. When your life is finished on this earth, that part of Christ's job is finished.

While jogging the other day, God told me something that made me stop running. He said, "Jesse, do you know that you've never lost a battle to the devil? The devil has never defeated you, and the devil cannot defeat you."

I said, "I don't want to shake the throne here, but let me show You where the boy (devil) knocked my socks off a few times."

But God said, "The devil didn't knock your socks off. How can he knock your socks off when he's under your feet? You are undefeatable. All of My people are undefeatable."

I asked, "What do You mean?"

He said, "Many have thought that they lost battles with the devil. The devil is under their feet. They lost the battle of faith. I told you to fight the good fight of faith. It's a good fight. The devil didn't beat you, you just quit fighting with faith."

I said, "It's hard, Lord. "

He said, "It' s not really hard if you are dealing in the realm of the Spirit. You have tried to get your flesh to fight the fight of faith. I told you to live by the faith of the Son of God, I didn't tell you to live by *your* faith. "

Paul said in Galatians 2: 20, *I am crucified with Christ: nevertheless I live; yet not I, but Christ liveth in me: and the life which I now live in the flesh I live by the faith of the Son of God, who loved me, and gave himself for me.*

Have you ever studied the faith of the Son of God? A living letter is more than a memory or an indication of what Christ did. It is living revelation of the Word of God. It is the power of the cross revealed in human flesh. When you live by the faith of the Son of God, you will truly be a living epistle, read by all men. You can't lose with that kind of faith.

> ### *The power of the cross is something that shines in the eyes, trembles in the voice, and throbs out of your every movement.*

Paul said, *For me to live is Christ* (Phil. 1:21). With his back bleeding, he and Silas sang about the goodness of God. Every fiber of his being throbbed with the fullness of Jesus Christ.

The power of the cross trembles in the voice. My wife, Cathy, used to hate to testify. She hated it because as soon as she'd start speaking, the tears would come gushing.

The pastor would ask, "Does anyone have a good testimony?" Most people didn't, but they stood up anyway. They'd say "The devil has been kicking my brains out. He hit me with a pick-up truck today, but I made it to church! Yeah, we lost our house. My husband got mad and shot the dog, the cat and tried to kill the kids but they just wouldn't die. "

Cathy would get up and begin, "I want to say...." She could never finish her testimony, she would always tremble, break down in the middle of it and cry. She would get so embarrassed.

That happens to many people. When the cross is so meaningful to you, it trembles in your voice and you become speechless.

The power of the cross is something that shines in the eyes. People can see it . You don't have to say a word to be a walking revelation of the Word of God.

I walked by a woman in the Atlanta airport who was rubbing the bottom of her leg. I could tell she was in pain. As I walked by, the Lord said, "Are you going to let that woman stay in pain?"

I said, "Yes, I don't know that lady. I'm just trying to get to that jet over there."

He said, "Are you a living epistle?"

I said, "Yes! "

He said, "Let her read you! "

I tried to reason with Him, "But, Lord, I'm going to miss my plane."

He said, "I'll hold it."

What are you going to do if God is holding a plane for you? You aren't going anywhere. I turned around and walked up to the lady and said, "Excuse me, madame, you don't know who I am, and that's all right, you don't need to know, but your leg is hurting and the Lord spoke to me and told me not to leave you sick and afflicted with that pain. IN JESUS' NAME BE HEALED!!"

Immediately, God touched her and she stood up and yelled, "It's working, I'm not hurting anymore! "

A Living Letter is a revelation of the Word of God.

How many times have you read the Bible and found it was only words? Before you were saved you probably thought the Bible was boring. The Word of God is only words unless it has a medium of expression.

Blotted, blurred or hard-to-read lives fail to communicate the message of your life to the reader. Some of you are barely-getting-by Christians. You compare the scars the devil put on you with other barely-getting-by Christians. You tell everyone what the devil's done to you, instead of what Jesus has done for you.

If you enjoy looking at each other's scars, you need prayer. There is a world around you dying and going to hell, and you've got the life jacket to save them.

Those in the world don't like people who are doubled-minded or wish-washy. To blow hot and cold with the same breath is an abomination to the world and the Word. James 3: 10 says, *Out of the same mouth proceedeth blessing and cursing. My brethren, these things ought not so to be.*

Christians should make the truth seem more true. We should make a lie seem more false. We should not only carry a message, we should be that message.

I hate it when people are overly interested in the details of my sinful past. I've had preachers say, "Brother Jesse, you've lived a pretty sinful life, haven't you? Being a musician, I'm sure you lived really bad, huh? I guess you've been around a lot of women... groupies, I mean. "

I'd say, "Yeah, I was pretty bad. "

They answer, " That's terrible, tell me about it. " They want to know! But I don't like to talk about what the devil has done. I like to talk about what Jesus has done!

When someone asks me to describe my past, they are basically telling me they don't hate sin, they like it. They hate what sin does to them, they hate the wages of sin, but they do not hate sin. If it tickles your ears and you enjoy hearing about it, you don't hate it. Sin is an attraction for some, and if they aren't careful, soon they will find themselves in it.

Do you know why people mess up in immorality? It is because they aren't wearing their underwear!

They talk about their helmet of salvation, their breastplate of righteousness and their sword of the Spirit. Their feet are shod with the preparation of the gospel of peace, but they never say anything about their loins being girded about with truth. That's what holds everything together! Your loins must be girded about with truth. If you are walking in truth, you will not sin. So put your underwear on and keep it on!

I believe the reason there are so many divorces in America is because we are not marrying women and men, we are marrying parts. We see parts and say, "Oooohh. Look at those parts." Let me make an announcement: Parts wear out!

Many people don't see their mates as persons; they see them only as a pile of parts. When some of those parts wear out, or when they just get tired of looking at them, they go to another part store.

Don't marry for looks. Eventually, it's all going to fall down. You need to marry someone because you love them. It doesn't matter if she has nine hundred varicose veins on her legs!

Once a man told me, "My wife's legs look like a United States map." I said, "What about all those red blood vessels on your nose? You look like you have interstates on your face! " Have you ever noticed when men start getting old, their noses start getting big and red, and lines start coming out on them.

I said, "If you want to look at parts, you better look at yours. What's the matter with you? You are running head on into sin. You are not an epistle of Jesus Christ; you are a stop sign! You aren't moving with the flow of Christ; you are stopping to try to find something." That man wasn't a living epistle, he was only interested in parts.

God created the first man and woman and called them Adam. God did not name Eve. Adam named Eve. When God created male and female he called them both Adam! He chose the female Adam to procreate. She was called woman, which means "man with a womb." God did not create Eve from Adam's foot, he created her from Adam's side! God made woman to stand side by side with a man to such a degree that their prayers would be hindered if they argued.

At the fall of man, God told Satan point blank that he would send one born of woman's seed that would bust his head. Women don't have seed, men have seed! For the birth of Jesus, God did not need a man. He needed man with womb; He needed a woman. That went right over Satan's head!

Ever since Satan died spiritually, he hasn't had a lick of sense! When you deal with the devil in the flesh, he will beat you, because he has years of experience. But, when you deal with him in the Spirit, like Jesus did, it totally confuses him. That is why it is so important to walk in the Spirit and fill yourself with the Word of God.

Throw scripture at him like Jesus did! "It is written, it is written, it is written." Jesus refused to take the devil out from under His feet. Satan did not understand what God told him in the garden until Jesus died, was resurrected and ascended. Then Satan said, "If we would have known, we never would have crucified Him!" Satan had been warned early on about one who would be born of woman's seed, yet he was too stupid to recognize Him when He came.

Throughout His life on earth, Jesus was a Living Letter to the world. John 1:1 says, *In the beginning was the Word, and the Word was with God, and the Word was God.*

Even in his death, Jesus was a living example of God's love to the world. After He was betrayed, ridiculed, beaten and nailed to a cruel cross, He prayed, *Father, forgive them; for they know not what they do* (Luke 23:34). It takes a great living letter to bless those who curse you, and pray for those who despitefully use you.

Chapter Three

Don't Be Affected By the World's Message

E ach day we are confronted with messages of death, destruction and lack. We live in a chaotic world filled with voices who invade us with unbelieving and disheartening words. They rattle on and on through television, radio, newspapers, and even our closest friends and family. Everywhere we turn we are given the opportunity to be affected by the world's message.

Ah, but this broken record has a flip side, a new song of deliverance! A song that will free us from the chains of circumstance and empower us to live victoriously no matter what the situation. However, the choice still remains ours. Will we sing along to the same old tune, or flip sides and learn a new song? It isn't hard, the words are right there in the book. All you have to do is pick it up and start practicing. *Death and life are in the power of the tongue: and they that love it shall eat the fruit thereof* (Prov. 18:21).

In the gospel of Luke we are introduced to Jairus, a ruler of the synagogue. Desperate and filled with anxiety over his only daughter's nearing death, he joined the multitude waiting to receive a miracle from Jesus Who was just returning from the country of the Gadarenes.

And it came to pass, that, when Jesus was returned, the people gladly received him: for they were all waiting for him.

And, behold, there came a man named Jairus, and he was ruler of the synagogue: and he fell down at Jesus' feet, and besought him that he would come into his house:

For he had one only daughter, about twelve years of age, and she lay a dying. But as he went the people thronged him (Luke 8:40-42).

Now Jairus was the ruler of the synagogue. By this time the rulers and high officials in the temple were strongly opposed to Jesus and His teachings. So much so that plans were being made to kill Him. You can imagine how Jairus must have felt as he fell to his knees and begged for a favor from Jesus, the very man his peers were planning to kill!

The scripture goes on, *And a woman having an issue of blood twelve years, which had spent all her living upon physicians, neither could be healed of any,*

Came behind him, and touched the border of his garment: and immediately her issue of blood stanched.

And Jesus said, Who touched me? When all denied, Peter and they that were with him said, Master, the multitude throng thee and press thee, and sayest thou, Who touched me?

And Jesus said, Somebody hath touched me: for I perceive that virtue is gone out of me.

And when the woman saw that she was not hid, she came trembling, and falling down before him, she declared unto him before all the people for what cause she had touched him, and how she was healed immediately.

And he said unto her, Daughter, be of good comfort: thy faith hath made thee whole; go in peace (Luke 8:43-48).

Isn't it just like a woman to be persistent and tenacious when she has a need? She didn't fall at His feet and beg for a miracle. She didn't even consult Him in the matter! She simply acted on her own faith in the divine healing power working in Jesus' life. Her faith actually drew the healing power out from Jesus without His being aware of her specific problem.

She put a demand on Jesus through faith, and she was made whole because of it.

It was an awesome miracle, but it wasn't helping Jairus. I can almost hear Jairus saying "My kid's dying right now! This woman's had her problem for twelve years! Can't He take care of her later? Let's go! "

The story continues, *While he yet spake, there cometh one from the ruler of the synagogue's house, saying to him, Thy daughter is dead; trouble not the Master.*

But when Jesus heard it, he answered him, saying, Fear not: believe only, and she shall be made whole (Luke 8:49,50).

When the messenger came, Jairus' heart sank. But Jesus, immediately upon hearing the bad report, chose not to be affected by it. He was full of faith that Jairus' daughter would live and be made whole regardless of the present circumstances. He told Jairus not to fear, but only to believe, and his daughter would be made whole. Fear is faith working in reverse, and faith is what Jairus would need to see his daughter alive and well.

And when he came into the house, he suffered no man to go in, save Peter, and James, and John, and the father and the mother of the maiden.

And all wept, and bewailed her: but he said, Weep not; she is not dead, but sleepeth (Luke 8:51,52).

Notice that Jesus allowed only Peter, James, John and the parents into the house with Him and the dead girl. Obviously others were trying to get in if He allowed only these few. I imagine that the rest of the disciples were saying, "I tell you one thing, I follow Jesus the same as those! I heard Peter cussing just last week, and I have to stay out here on the porch!"

The mourning crowd mocked and laughed at Him for claiming that the girl was sleeping. They knew that Jairus' daughter was dead. She'd probably been dead for a while before Jesus was even able to get there. Yet again, Jesus was not affected by the message of the girl's death, the fear in Jairus, the angry disciples or the laughing mourners. He refused to be affected by what the world was doing and saying around Him.

And he put them all out, took her by the hand, and called, saying, Maid, arise.

And her spirit came again, and she arose straightway: and he commanded to give her meat.

And her parents were astonished: but he charged them that they should tell no man what was done (Luke 8:54-56).

Notice that Jesus was not interested in the spectacular. He charged the parents not to tell anyone. Today, if someone was raised from the dead, every TV camera in America would be on the scene saying, "okay, make the dead person do something. Let's see how it works. " But Jesus wasn't interested in the publicity the miracle would bring Him. He was interested in seeing the afflicted healed.

Jesus never said, "I have the gift of miracles and the gift of healing." He had God, and because He had God, He had all that too. He said, *Believest thou not that I am in the Father, and the Father in me? the words that I speak unto you I speak not of myself: but the Father that dwelleth in me, he doeth the works* (John 14:10).

Don 't allow the world to affect your spirit.

Your spirit must take precedence over the situation. First John 4:4 says, *Greater is he that is in you, than he that is in the world.* No matter what the situation is, God is greater. He lives inside of you, and faith in Him will enable you to overcome any situation. Don't deny how bad your situation is, refuse to be affected by it.

People ask me about the Louisiana recession and wonder if I am being hurt by it. I just tell them that we're not participating in it. Other evangelists have told me that December and January are the worst months for ministries financially. They say people are involved with the holidays, go on vacation and forget that they are your partner. Yet those months continue to be some of our best!

People enjoy being our Covenant Partners, and they find it a privilege to join with a ministry that is helping to bring the lost to Christ! Recently, someone came up to me all excited and said, "Jesse Duplantis! I'm your partner!" I was so blessed I said, "Isn't it wonderful, you and me getting people saved, linked up together!"

God said He will supply my need according to His riches in glory. (Phil. 4: 19.) He said if I doubt not in my heart but believe that those things that I say will come to pass, they will!

For verily I say unto you, That whosoever shall say unto this mountain, Be thou removed, and be thou cast into the sea; and shall not doubt in his heart, but shall believe that those things which he saith shall come to pass; he shall have whatsoever he saith (Mark 11:23).

God didn't tell us to go up on the mountain, get spiritually crazy on it, build a camp up there and pray over it all day, every day. He said it pretty simple. Just don't doubt, believe it and say it. Your faith will move that mountain in your life.

Don't deny your problems, deny their rights!

Don't deny the existence of a mountain in your life, deny its authority to stay and refuse to allow it to stop the plan of God in your life. Don't be affected by the world's message.

If you have a tumor as big as a basketball, it's hard to deny. But you can deny its right to be in your body. Your spirit must take precedence over the situation.

That's what Jesus did with Jairus. He made it clear that even if He was late in getting to his home, the girl would be made whole. And to be "whole," she would have to be alive. She wouldn't stay dead, no matter what the message was.

Once a man came up to me who was crying and complaining about circumstances with his family that he experienced over thirty years ago. He said, "I come from a dysfunctional family, I have so many problems, I don't know what to do."

I looked at him and said, "You are still talking about stuff that happened thirty years ago? If you are saved, then it is passed away, what are you trying to remind God for? Did He give you a new heart, a new spirit? Then walk in your given power! You are a new creature in Christ Jesus! The Bible says to forget those things which are behind and reach out to those things that are ahead."

It's ridiculous to keep dredging up the past so you can weep over it again and again. You can't change what happened in your past. Forgive those who have wronged you and release it! The Word commands us to do so. Who didn't come from a dysfunctional family? Unless your entire family was born again with the full knowledge of the power of God living and working inside them, you came from a dysfunctional family! It's time to quit living in the past, because the past never sees the future. Make up your mind, if Jesus is real and His Word is truth, then it ought to work in your life.

The scorner will produce the truth by natural law, but God will produce the truth by divine spiritual law.

In Jairus' case, the message was of death. But Jesus wasn't worried about the natural law. He was moving through the power of divine spiritual law. The spirit is much more powerful than the physical body or anything in the natural. The body can't live without the spirit, but the spirit can live without the body.

So if the doctors give you a negative report concerning your physical body, do not allow the message to come in and steal your faith. Remember that your spirit is stronger than your body, and God promised, *With long life will I satisfy him, and shew him my salvation* (Ps. 91:16). Your faith will make you whole, so fear not and only believe. You have a better, more qualified Physician living right on the inside of you. He is well able to make you whole and the only payment accepted for His services is faith in His abilities. *Who hath believed our report? and to whom is the arm of the Lord revealed?* (Isa. 53:1).

The Word clearly says that we will have troubles in this life. It is how we handle them that will make us victorious. Proverbs 18:21 says, *Death and life are in the power of the tongue: and they that love it shall eat the fruit thereof.* The choice is again yours. Will you choose life or will your choose death? Since the power is in your words, you must be cautious to elevate the answer, not the problem.

Don't be affected by the world's message. Be affected only by what Jesus and His Word says. If you will believe, trust in, adhere and rely on Him, your miracle will come to pass. Your mountain will be removed.

With faith and patience, you will inherit the promises of God! Remember, you are not of this world, so why choose to be affected by the circumstances in it?

Chapter Four

Never Let Them See You Sweat

The devil is on the limits of retardation! He is so spiritually dead that he can only work in the realm of the flesh. His aim is to bind you with fear and keep you sweating with worry all the days of your life. That's why the devil tries to get you to believe his lies instead of the Word of God. His tactics are old and weak, but your weapons are mighty through God for the pulling down of strongholds. All you have to do is put on the armor of God, stand on the Word and never let him see you sweat.

I love to surprise the devil and mess up his plans for my defeat. I can't help it, I'm possessed! I am possessed with a Holy Spirit, so powerful that it keeps me at peace in the midst of strong opposition.

Jonathan, son of King Saul, was the same way. He was possessed to wage war on the enemies of God. He didn't care how many were against him or how invincible the enemy appeared to be. He was a man who was totally possessed with victory at any cost.

First Samuel chapter 13 tells us how the army of Israel was greatly outnumbered by the Philistines which were camped at Michmash. The Hebrews were so terrified that they were literally trembling in fear as they scattered in every direction from the army of the Philistines, and hid themselves in caves, in thickets, in cliffs, in cellars and in pits. (Verse 6.)

And then 1 Samuel 14:6,7 says, *Jonathan said to the young man that bare his armour, Come, and let us go over unto the garrison of these uncircumcised: it may be that the Lord will work for us: for there is no restraint to the Lord to save by many or by few.*

And his armour-bearer said unto him, Do all that is in thine heart: turn thee; behold, I am with thee according to thy heart.

Jonathan was possessed with the idea of attacking the Philistines. It didn't make a lick of difference how many were against him or how difficult the path, he never let them see him sweat. He had hope, faith, inspiration and daring effort as he climbed over sharp rocks to the garrison of the Philistines.

When they saw Jonathan and his armor-bearer, they said, *Behold, the Hebrews come forth out of the holes where they had hid themselves.*

And the men of the garrison answered Jonathan and his armour-bearer, and said, Come up to us, and we will shew you a thing. And Jonathan said unto his armour-bearer, Come up after me: for the Lord hath delivered them into the hand of Israel.

And Jonathan climbed up upon his hands and upon his feet, and his armour-bearer after him: and they fell before Jonathan; and his armour-bearer slew after him.

And that first slaughter, which Jonathan and his armour-bearer made, was about twenty men, within as it were an half acre of land, which a yoke of oxen might plow.

And there was trembling in the host, in the field, and among all the people: the garrison, and the spoilers, they also trembled, and the earth quaked: so it was a very great trembling.

And the watchmen of Saul in Gibeah of Benjamin looked; and, behold, the multitude melted away, and they went on beating down one another (1 Sam. 14: 11-16).

Victory was won because someone had hope that God would fight their battle and faith that He was not restrained to save by many or by few.

Hope starts out first, and faith finishes the course.

In order to win, we need to have a blueprint, a plan. Ideas grow in power over us when we nourish them, brood over our thoughts and purpose by the aid of the Spirit of God. Never be faithless to any conviction given to you by God.

Jonathan's conviction was so strong that it possessed him. He knew that it wasn't his project to be carried out; it was the Lord's cause to be advanced.

Inspiration shields the faithful and works the wonders of redemption. The life of a true man or woman of God is crowded with evidence of divine inspiration. Jonathan became inspired when he realized that he was dealing with uncircumcised people who didn't have a covenant with God. The only thing they had was their own physical strength, but he had a covenant with Jehovah that could not be broken.

The height of wisdom is to give God the opportunity to reveal His mighty arm. We are not serving some wimp God! He is powerful and likes doing things in a big way. At the Red Sea, He blew His nose, and the sea parted! The Bible says with a blast of His nostrils, the water took off. He could have put His hand down to separate the sea, but He blew His nose.

Jonathan's defeat of the Philistines was theatrical. Hope and faith worked to produce strong inspiration which convinced his armor-bearer to follow him in the Lord's cause.

Daring effort is a must even if it means great risk.

God gives us strength according to our requirements. Though the might is God's, the daring, will and effort are ours.

Jonathan knew the might was the Lord's, therefore it didn't matter to him if he had to fight two or two thousand. However, nothing would have happened until Jonathan's will lined up with God's will. He had to link daring effort with his faith-filled words before victory could be realized.

We must stand up and exercise daring effort to be a part of the great harvest that is before us. Revival will not come easily, for it is a campaign waged against the world, the flesh and the devil. Abortion clinics scream at revival. Bar rooms and honky tonks scream at revival. Prostitution houses scream at revival. Crime, drugs and booze scream at revival.

The need for revival is great, but our God is not restrained to save by many or by few. You can kick out any evil in the area around you, because greater is He that is in you than he that is in the world. It will take hope, faith, inspiration and daring effort, but true revival will come. Its influences will be felt all across our land. Jesus is coming for a church without spot or wrinkle, full of faith and power.

Chapter Five

The Valley of "Ono"

Everyone is familiar with the expression, "Oh, no!" When something goes wrong, or we get into trouble, the first thing we say is, "Oh, no! " Many of you may have trouble so deep, it feels like you are living in the valley of "Ono."

It's true that trouble will come in this life. Jesus said we would have tribulation, but He would enable us to overcome it. With love, faith and zeal, God can empower us to travel through the valley of "Ono" without a scratch.

Nehemiah, a cupbearer for the king in the palace in Shushan, was quite familiar with peril. Just like you and me, he'd traveled through the valley of "Ono" more than once. Yet Nehemiah never chose to stay very long. He relied upon his faith in a loving and merciful Father to get him through the valley of "Ono" every time.

One day men traveling from Judah brought Nehemiah some terrible news from Jerusalem. The children of Israel were in great affliction, the wall of Jerusalem was broken down, and its gates were burned.

When Nehemiah heard this news he cried, "Oh, no!" He wept and mourned, fasted and fervently prayed for days. He cried out to God for mercy and forgiveness for the sins of the nation. In turn, God gave him a vision to rebuild the wall and restore the people.

After receiving permission and supplies from the king, he went to Jerusalem to fulfill his vision. When he arrived and surveyed the extensive damage, he had yet another opportunity to cry, "Oh, no!" Instead he gathered the people and shared his vision.

As the people prepared for the work that was ahead, the surrounding nations laughed and scorned them. They said it couldn't be done.

Did you ever notice that when people get in the realm of the impossible, that's when things start to happen?

When everybody says it can't be done, God has an opportunity to produce a manifestation for the world to see.

Nehemiah, confident in the love of God, focused on his vision and began to rebuild the wall. While the people of Israel worked together, their enemies continued to mock them, conspiring together to fight against Jerusalem and hinder the building.

Now it came to pass, when Sanballat, and Tobiah, and Geshem the Arabian, and the rest of our enemies, heard that I had builded the wall, and that there was no breach left therein; (though at that time I had not set up the doors upon the gates;)

That Sanballat and Geshem sent unto me, saying, Come, let us meet together in some one of the villages in the plain of Ono. But they thought to do me mischief.

And I sent messengers unto them, saying, I am doing a great work, so that I cannot come down: why should the work cease, whilst I leave it, and come down to you?

Yet they sent unto me four times after this sort; and I answered them after the same manner (Neh. 6: 1-4).

Nehemiah knew that the valley of "Ono" meant trouble for him. But instead of cowering in fear, he prayed, set up watch and continued building.

Has God ever told you to do something and you said, "Oh, no!" Has He ever told you to invite your father and mother to your church when they already think you're crazy?

You've invited them regularly for years. You've prayed for God to get them there, save them, touch them and bless them so they won't go to hell. Finally, one Sunday morning they walk in the door of your church and first thing you say is, "Oh, no!" Next you are praying, "Okay God, don't let that crazy man jump up and speak in tongues. Oh, and God, get rid of Sister So-n-so. You know when she speaks in tongues she just drools all over everybody."

What you are really asking God for is a nice, calm, dead service. Then the first thing you try to do is prepare your parents for the worst when you should be preparing them for the best. But you don't need to make excuses for God or His ways. Remember, they were originally created to serve God. His Holy Spirit will use the love and power of God ministering life to the people in that church to tug on their hearts.

When God tells you He wants you to do something, He wants you to give your all. You must commit, discipline and dedicate yourself to the work.

Don't say, "Oh, God, I don't want to do that. "If you disobey, you are working against God instead of working for God. You begin to take on the nature of Satan through your disobedience to God. The reason most people say "Oh, no!" is because they have never crucified their flesh to receive the fullness of the teaching the Holy Ghost wants to give.

Don't be swayed from trusting in God just because you are in the valley of "Ono"! He's with you always, even when you're in the valley. You may not feel Him, but He is there.

So many times people try to feel or touch God in the realm of the five senses. They try to reach out to God and say, "Lord, I didn't feel You today. Would You touch me one more time?" But as you grow in the power and Spirit of the living God, you begin to grow beyond the realm of touch. You begin to grow beyond the realm of the five physical senses. You begin to grow in the light of God's Word, and even when you don't feel God and you're in the valley of "Ono" thinking, "God, do You know where I am?" Jesus said, "I'll never leave you nor forsake you." (Heb. 13:5.) He's with you every minute of your life.

I decided years ago to believe the whole Bible, quit being God's opponent and walk in the flow of the Holy Ghost. Until then, I never realized God would take a Cajun boy from South Louisiana and call him to preach all over the world.

One time I was preaching and the anointing of God was upon me. In front of 4,000 people, the wind hit my notes and blew my page over. I didn't notice it and read a point on another message. It didn't make any more sense than the man on the moon. I was talking about the love of God and all of a sudden I read, "You must sanctify yourselves. "

I said to myself, "This isn't making any sense. " I preached the rest of a whole other sermon and never knew it. Over three hundred people got saved that night.

When I got back to the hotel I said, "God, that was trash, nothing seemed to fit."

God reminded me of the three hundred who'd given their lives to Him that night.

I told Him, "You must have clogged their ears, because what I said didn't make any sense. Oh no, it was terrible."

God told me to look at my notes.

I looked at them and said, " I didn't preach that tonight . "

He said, "The wind blew over the page, and I thought it was the funniest thing. "

I said, "God, You could have told me something."

He replied, "Tell you what, I enjoyed it."

So now I take paper clips with me, because I don't want any more "Oh, no's. "

Jude 1:21 says, *Keep yourselves in the love of God, looking for the mercy of our Lord Jesus Christ unto eternal life.*

You keep yourself in the love of God by blessing those who despitefully use you and curse you.

When people are walking in the love of God, God's plan is formed and manifested.

God wants us to look for mercy instead of judgment. Instead of condemning those in sin and putting judgment on them, give them mercy so that they can come out of that valley of "Ono" and be a blessing for God. Judgment will only push them away, love and mercy will draw them close.

Once I was preaching in an outdoor meeting, and a guy came up to the platform and spit right in my face. "That's what I think about your Gospel of Jesus," he said. That spit was just dripping off my face, and the more it dripped the madder I got.

I said, "Lord, You need to save this boy, because his rear end is mine. "

Then the Lord reminded me, "Keep yourself in My love. "

I said, "I'm going to kick his head off. Look at this spit in my face, God! "

He said, "They spit in Mine too. That's nothing new, show Me something else. Show Me the scars in your hands. Show Me your pierced side. Show Me your sweat drops of blood. You think you've been in the valley of 'Ono,' I've been to the Garden of Gethsemane for you. "

I looked at that boy and said, "Son, I'm sorry."

He said, "What did you do?"

I said, "I was thinking bad thoughts. Forgive me." It shook him.

Then the devil said, "He's going to spit on the other side. "

I said, "Let him spit, I'll just get a cloth and wipe it off."

That boy got on his knees on the street corner and gave his heart to Jesus.

Now, had I chosen to start fighting him, there would have been little chance of his salvation. But by keeping in the love of God I was able to see God's plan at work. A life was transformed and set free simply because I chose to keep myself in the love of God.

People full of faith are also full of power.

One single soul (mind, will and emotions) animated by faith, love and zeal can defeat all the agencies of the evil one. Psalm 8:2 says, *Out of the mouth of babes and sucklings hast thou ordained strength because of thine enemies, that thou mightest still the enemy and the avenger.* Even a baby Christian, if animated by faith, love and zeal will defeat any agency Satan has.

However, most baby Christians are defeated by older Christians. The adolescent Christian comes up and says, "Look, man, right now you are going high, but you are going to come down to where we are pretty soon. You need to be with us in gloom and despair."

Don't listen! If you will make a commitment to be of good cheer, full of faith in every circumstance, the tribulation will cease. You'll have so much fun having trouble that the devil will stop giving you trouble! Your cheer will totally exhaust your trouble. You'll be full of cheer, full of faith and full of the power of God!

Jesus' Garden of Gethsemane was His valley of "Ono." Daniel's valley of "Ono" was the lion's den. The three Hebrew children's fiery furnace was their valley of "Ono." All of them were overcomers, because they would not let the valley of "Ono" stop them from standing full of faith, love and zeal.

The best defense against temptation is to be pledged to a positive, biblical life of active service.

The Holy Spirit inside of you is always in opposition to the spirit of compromise. If you are pledged to touching the lost for Jesus, it will be hard for you to stay in the valley of "Ono."

When the spirit of compromise says, "You can't do that," the Holy Spirit inside of you says, "Heal the sick, raise the dead and cast out devils. " If you have pledged yourself to a positive, biblical life of active service, the temptation in the valley of "Ono" will never overthrow you.

Temptation is a trap set by Satan to make you fall into a life of compromise. It is one of the main tactics he uses to chip away at your convictions and bind the Holy Ghost's power inside of you from fulfilling God's ultimate plan for your life.

Satan will try desperately to destroy your effectiveness as a born-again, Spirit-filled believer. He knows that if he can get you to compromise your pledge to a life of positive, biblical, active service for God, you won't be very effective in winning the lost. It's his plan to have you living an inactive Christian life, full of negativity and compromise.

However, if you are living an active, positive, biblical life of service, he won't be able to catch you in the trap. You won't be tantalized by the devil's cheese. You'll know that it' s rotten to the core, and it's equipped with a deadly blade.

James 1:22 says, *But be ye doers of the word, and not hearers only, deceiving your own selves.* The Bible says that the just shall *live* by faith, not *try* by faith. Be a doer, not a trier. Stand firm in the conviction of the work. Be pledged to a life of active service.

The valley of "Ono" is where an individual realizes his place, his consecration, his strength and his ability in the Kingdom of God.

In the Garden of Gethsemane, Jesus said, *Abba, Father, all things are possible unto thee; take away this cup from me: nevertheless not what I will, but what thou wilt* (Mark 14: 36).

Daniel, the statesman, after being delivered from the lion's den said to the king, *My God hath sent his angel, and hath shut the lions' mouths, that they have not hurt me: forasmuch as before him innocency was found in me; and also before thee, O king, have I done no hurt* (Dan. 6:22).

The three Hebrew children didn't even smell the smoke when they were thrown into the fiery furnace.

Just like Nehemiah, all of these believers realized their places in the Kingdom of God. They were all consecrated to God's Kingdom and His will for their individual lives, and so they found strength and ability in the Kingdom of God.

Don't let the troubles in the valley of "Ono" destroy you. Allow Jesus to show you the way out. Don't fight the devil; resist him steadfastly in the faith. He must bow at the name of Jesus, he has no other choice. It's the greatest thing in the world to look at the devil when you've stood strong in faith and hear him say, "We must retreat, he refuses to fight me."

Chapter Six

Standing in the Strength of God

$\mathbf{D}$o you know how to stand in the strength of God? Do you rely on your own strength, the strength of theology, or the strength of Jesus? The Bible exhorts us to be strong in the Lord, yet many Christians have never learned how to stand in the strength of God.

Ephesians 6: 10-18 says, *Finally, my brethren, be strong in the Lord, and in the power of his might.*

Put on the whole armour of God, that ye may be able to stand against the wiles of the devil.

For we wrestle not against flesh and blood, but against principalities, against powers, against the rulers of the darkness of this world, against spiritual wickedness in high places.

Wherefore take unto you the whole armour of God, that ye may be able to withstand in the evil day, and having done all, to stand.

Stand therefore, having your loins girt about with truth, and having on the breastplate of righteousness;

And your feet shod with the preparation of the gospel of peace;

Above all, taking the shield of faith, wherewith ye shall be able to quench all the fiery darts of the wicked.

And take the helmet of salvation, and the sword of the Spirit, which is the word of God:

Praying always with all prayer and supplication in the Spirit, and watching thereunto with all perseverance and supplication for all saints.

Our struggle is not against flesh and blood. Our struggle is against rulers, powers, and forces of darkness. There are different kinds of devils just as there are different kinds of angels, but the devil doesn't have anything new. The same things he tricked Eve with are what he uses today. We must be wise enough to stand against the schemes of the devil and not each other.

We fight God when we fight each other, because we are fighting the same spirit that should be bearing witness with the Holy Spirit. When we stand in God's strength, we are on alert for the Body of Christ. Instead of helping the devil tear down the Body, we completely quench his flaming missiles with the light of God.

The strength of God is joy, and the joy of the Lord is your strength. If you are standing in the strength of God, joy should be evident in your life.

Some people attribute the growth of my ministry to my personality. They say, "You are an exciting individual. You know how to stir people up!" They believe that my personality has opened up doors for me. The truth is that the Lord Jesus Christ opens up the doors as I stand in His strength.

I never stand in my own strength; I can't handle it. Jesus said to His disciples, *Watch and pray, that ye enter not into temptation: the spirit indeed is willing, but the flesh is weak* (Matt. 26:41). So I don't stand in the realm of the flesh; I crucify it daily and stand in the strength of God.

People fall to the wayside if they stand in their own strength. Some burn out because they take the cares and responsibilities of this world upon themselves. They go to the altar, bawl and squall saying, "Lord, I'm giving this to You," and on their way out they pick it back up. They go by what they see instead of what Jesus said.

Some people say that if you don't "feel" God, then He isn't around. That's not true. If you believe that, then you are standing in your own strength.

Once, I went for months without hearing from God. I said, "Lord, I'm in the valley of dry bones. " I checked my soul. I checked my spirit. I checked my body. I did everything I knew to get God to speak to me and still nothing.

Soon the devil started to put accusations in my mind. I started thinking, "What did I do wrong?"

Finally, the Lord spoke and said, "Hi, Jess! " It was so refreshing.

I said, "I hadn't heard from You in so long, I thought You had moved."

He said, "Shout, boy, you are growing! "

"Growing? I've been in a valley."

He said, "You've been on a mountaintop for months."

"I didn't feel You or see You or hear You."

He said, "Ain't that nice?"

"No, that ain't nice. Why wouldn't You talk to me?"

He said, "Jesse, you know My Word. There will be times that I will pat you on the back and tell you I love you three or four times a day. Yet there will be times I may not. That doesn't mean I don't love you or that I'm not there. Remember, the less you feel Me, the more you grow. You will begin to live more in the Spirit and less in the flesh."

When Cathy and I first got married, she would never go to sleep without me. Now she says, "See you later, Jack. " There isn't anything wrong with that, she is sleepy, and I might be studying or doing something else. Our marriage stands in its own strength, so if I don't kiss Cathy every day before I leave, the house doesn't fall down.

Have you ever driven in a car behind a newly married couple? You can only see one head! As the years go by, you could drive a Mack truck through them and never touch the sides. I'm not saying that you grow apart. You actually love each other more with time, you simply become more stable and secure in your love for each other.

There are many people looking for the shout to produce the light instead of letting the light produce the shout.

They think emotion and excitement will produce light in them. The light of God is available to us right now. We don't need to shout, scream and beg to get it. All we need to do is put on the armor of light, and the light will produce the shout.

Romans 13: 12 says, *The night is far spent, the day is at hand: let us therefore cast off the works of darkness, and let us put on the armour of light.* The armor of light on you blinds Satan. Light comes from all around, and he can't tell whether it's you or God. Don't turn off the light and begin to stand in your own strength.

I've heard people say, "Bless God, if it kills me, I'm going to get healed." Well, you are going to die, because you are standing in your own strength. Strength comes from God, not from the way you do things. It's the Father in you who should do the work.

Jesus said, *I can of mine own self do nothing: as I hear, I judge: and my judgment is just; because I seek not mine own will, but the will of the Father which hath sent me* (John 5:30). Again in the Garden of Gethsemane He said, *Father. . . not my will, but thine, be done* (Luke 22:42).

Jesus did not enjoy the terrible things that were done to Him. He was punched in the face and spit on. His beard was pulled out and a crown of thorns was placed on His head. A scarlet cloak was thrown over Him and they kicked dust in His face and mocked Him. He didn't like any of that, but He did it so that you and I could have this glorious life of redemption.

In the midst of spit, blood, cursing and degradation, He said, *Father, forgive them; for they know not what they do* (Luke 23:34). Jesus was standing in the strength of His Father.

There have been times I've thought I'd hung on a cross. I've had people wag their heads at me, spit, scream and holler. I've had people pull knives on me. My first thoughts were, "I could have stayed home. I don't need this mess. I don't have to put up with this trash."

The Lord said, "Preach the Gospel. " So I stood in the strength of God. Now my flesh didn't like it, but that' s all right. My flesh will never like anything I do when it comes to the Spirit of God. Romans 7: 18 says, *For I know that in me (that is, in my flesh,) dwelleth no good thing: for to will is present with me; but how to perform that which is good I find not.* So instead of trying to appease my flesh, I just crucify it daily.

Whatever you preach, you should produce.

You can talk your talk, but what is going to happen when the test comes? Anyone can get angry and sin. Your flesh wants to sin. You might get aggravated and feel like your wife is running you up a tree. You think, "That's it, Jack, I'm gonna get me a bottle of booze and slowly slide down this tree. " That's when you must crucify your flesh and say, "No, I'll not do that, in the name of Jesus." Does your confession become your possession? Whatever you preach, you should produce.

I was in the Atlanta airport and the devil was really irritating me. I was standing in line waiting for my ticket, and the devil injected trash into my head, so I said out loud, "Get out of here. "

I made another step forward in line and he continued to put thoughts in my mind. Finally, I just had enough and I yelled, "No, I'll not do it."

The people in line looked at me and said, "Go ahead up to the front there, it's all right."

I said, "I have had enough of the devil. I'll have nothing to do with the devil at all." It just came out of my mouth. I was angry, and my righteous indignation was showing!

One man looked at me and asked, "Is the devil getting on this plane?" He didn't know what to think.

God said to me, "Well, Jesse, you found out how strong you've become. It's a blessing to Me when My people get angry at the devil."

The Bible says, *And from the days of John the Baptist until now the kingdom of heaven suffereth violence, and the violent take it by force* (Matt. 11:12). The devil will never give you anything, you have to take it out of his hand.

It's easy to get down on yourself. I got a case of the mullygrubs once. I was in a hotel room by myself, and I began to feel sorry for myself. "You've been traveling, always away from your family. God's got you in these hotels all the time, " I thought to myself.

The devil started to help me out. He said, "You are a good ole boy, I wonder why God runs you so hard?"

I said, "I don't know. " I began to get angry, and I said, "I ought to let them all go to hell, I don't even need to preach tonight."

Finally, the Lord spoke to me, and He said, "Well, why don't you just go on home? I'll have somebody else fill this hotel room and the pulpit tonight. You think you are lonely? I'll never leave you nor forsake you, but how many times have you disobeyed Me?"

I said, "I'm sorry, Lord. Devil, get out of here. "

The Lord said, "Now repent, turn from it and go the other way. Besides, I'm paying for this hotel room. Now get out of here and go do something for Me."

I hit that front door and started walking down the street, looking for someone I could preach to. I went into a restaurant and found someone. You know God will always have someone ready to receive the Gospel if you are ready to proclaim it.

Truth will sustain you in God's Word because strength is developed by truth.

Ephesians 6:14 says, *Stand therefore, having your loins girt about in truth.* Truth will produce strength in the believer. God's Word is the truth that gives us the faith to follow Jesus.

A person who does not read the Bible is in the same position as the person who cannot read. They are perishing due to a lack of knowledge.

I've told many people, "If you stand on the Word of God, God's Word will come to pass."

They say to me, "I've tried that stuff, and it doesn't work."

I remind them that Hebrews 10:38 says, *The just shall live by faith.* Not try by faith. You are not going to try to go to work tomorrow, you will.

The only way to stand in the strength of God is to spend time with Him. This intimate fellowship with Jesus will sustain you through any storm this life may bring. You don't have to stand alone in desperate situations, weakened by life's disappointments. God's strength is available for all.

Come unto me, all ye that labour and are heavy laden, and I will give you rest (Matt. 11:28).

Chapter Seven

Songs in the Night

Have you ever felt beaten up, like the world's against you? Instead of complaining and pouting about it, try praying and singing praises to God. That's what Paul and Silas did when they were put in prison for doing the work of Jesus. They were down, but they never lost their joy.

And when her masters saw that the hope of their gains was gone, they caught Paul and Silas, and drew them into the marketplace unto the rulers,

And brought them to the magistrates, saying, These men, being Jews, do exceedingly trouble our city,

And teach customs, which are not lawful for us to receive, neither to observe, being Romans.

And the multitude rose up together against them: and the magistrates rent off their clothes, and commanded to beat them.

And when they had laid many stripes upon them, they cast them into prison, charging the jailor to keep them safely:

Who, having received such a charge, thrust them into the inner prison, and made their feet fast in the stocks.

And at midnight Paul and Silas prayed, and sang praises unto God: and the prisoners heard them (Acts 16:19-25).

I'm not saying that you should be happy about your problems. I don't think Paul and Silas were saying, "Thank you for beating us up and throwing us in prison." They were hurting, but they chose to look at their Savior instead of their pain. They sang songs in the night.

Faith gives you the ability to sing in all sorts of difficult and devastating circumstances.

It's not easy, but it's a command of God to walk by faith. In order to truly do that, we must get rid of despondent thoughts. Second Corinthians 10:5 instructs us to bring every thought into captivity to the obedience of Christ. *Casting down imaginations, and every high thing that exalteth itself against the knowledge of God, and bringing into captivity every thought to the obedience of Christ.*

If we didn't have the ability to do that, God never would have recorded it in scripture. How do we knock down and destroy despondent thoughts? By trusting Jesus, the Author and Finisher of our faith and singing songs in the night.

I travel hundreds of thousands of miles a year preaching the Gospel of Jesus. Many flights are uneventful, but one was a particularly difficult and potentially devastating circumstance.

Everyone boarded the plane and we took off. As the plane began climbing in the air, things started to go wrong. I didn't know what was happening, but by the looks on the flight attendants' faces, something was definitely up.

We got to the right altitude and the plane leveled out in the air. Things seemed to be going all right when all of a sudden I heard something go, "Baddoom!" Something on that plane exploded! The people went nuts! They were screaming and hollering as the flight attendants ran down the aisles trying to calm everyone. The plane started going down! It seemed slow at first, but then I began feeling the force of going down. My body said, "This is it, boy! This is the big one. Kiss yourself good-bye!"

We were all in a terrible situation. Almost immediately my spirit took control and I said, "Bless God, before I die, I'm going to get someone saved by the power of Jesus. "

I began to pray and shout. I said, "How many of y'all need to know Jesus?" All of them said, "Oh, yes! " (You can get people saved in an airplane crash.)

I said, "Just say this real quick, 'Jesus, forgive my sins and come into my life.'" They all said it, it was wonderful! It knocked out all fear, and we prayed for a miracle. Thank God the plane landed, and we all survived. Glory!

Now I could have had despondent thoughts about dying or wondering what would happen to my ministry, but instead I sang a song in the night, and God was glorified.

Paul and Silas, in the midst of their terrible circumstance, sang a song in the night. It may have been midnight physically, but it was morning in their souls. Their faith gave them the ability to see beyond their circumstances.

Our unseen audience is one of life's most familiar facts.

Paul and Silas had an unseen audience: the prisoners heard them. The jailhouse where Paul and Silas were held was for criminals, but their songs sanctified that place of cruelty. The evidence is in the fact that when the earthquake came and made a way for escape, no one left.

The criminals had a chance to be free but stayed. They were shocked, not by the earthquake, but by the songs and praises. They were astonished by the men who were not cursing the jailor, instead they were praying for him.

If something is terribly wrong in your life right now, it's time to start singing! Even if you don't feel like it, make a joyful noise of praise to God. An unseen audience may hear you and be changed forever.

One time I was traveling to a meeting, I was seated between two men on the plane. I don't usually like to sit in the middle seat, because I hate to elbow wrestle for the armrest. However, I was in a really good mood, and didn't mind the inconvenience.

While waiting quietly for the plane to take off, my eyes caught the eyes of the guy next to me. Just at that moment, I started speaking in tongues. The man just stared at me in wonder.

I asked him, "Did you hear that?"

He said, "Yeah! "

I said, "Mister, you just heard God talk. "

He looked at me and said, "Wow! Is that tongues?"

"Yes," I answered.

"Do it again," he said.

I said, "I can't do it again. It ain't me talking, it's God talking. Mister, you just heard God talk. "

All of a sudden, I started doing it again and the man said, "There He goes again."

By that time I was stirred up, and I looked at the man on the other side of me and asked, "Do you know Jesus?"

He looked over at me and said, "No, but it looks like I'm going to find out about Him."

God knows there are always people watching and listening even when we don't even notice they are there. Christians need to bring the power of the Holy Spirit everywhere they go.

Our business is to make happiness for others. We should light fires in cold rooms, chase the clouds away and scatter gloom.

Once I met a guy in a wheelchair whose speech was very impaired. He wanted to speak to me desperately, but I was having a hard time understanding him. As I listened a little longer, I began to understand him. At the end of our conversation, he said, "Thank you."

His mother looked at me and said, "No one ever talks to him. He loves God, and he loves you. You make him laugh, because you know a Jesus Who is happy."

I know Jesus had to have a sense of humor, especially with those twelve boys on His staff. Eleven of them could not work for me. Peter would slap you, cuss you, punch you and then pray for you. He was a tough man. John, the apostle of love, once got so mad at a whole city, he wanted to call fire down from heaven and burn the place. Jesus said, "Hey son, I didn't come to kill anybody."

Jesus was a person Who sang songs in the night. On the cross, bleeding and hurting, He did not say, "God, kill them."

He said, "Father, forgive them, for they don't know not what they're doing." Jesus made happiness for others.

That is our business, as well, to make happiness for others. Have you ever walked into a room that was cold, and people were depressed? Did you chase away the gloom? Did you light a fire and say, "Jesus Christ can minister gloriously today!"

It is always more blessed to give than to receive. You never know the true worth of something until you share it with others. We must share the truth of Jesus Christ with those around us. Sometimes the only way to do that is to sing a song in the night and let your light shine. Suddenly, cold rooms will light up with the love of Jesus.

So, if you are believing God for your husband to be saved, don't beat him in the head. Pray for him and love him and sing a song in the night.

Men are not going to be argued into goodness. They are going to be won into it. You cannot be lectured into the Kingdom, you must be called by the Holy Spirit.

People get mad when you tell them that they are going to hell. Most will say, "I know I'm going to hell. " Some will tell you they like hell. We shouldn't attack people for what they are doing, just let them see Jesus. Zeal is great, but without wisdom, you know only enough to be dangerous. We must not try to change people, only God can do that.

While sitting on another plane, a man came in with two little girls. They were about four and nine years old, and they sat right next to me. He hugged them really tight and he said, "Okay, your mom is going to meet you. Don't worry about anything, the stewardess is going to take care of you. Daddy loves you. "

The little nine-year-old started to cry softly. The four-year-old looked over, saw her sister and began to cry too. The father got up and walked out, trying to hold it together.

The little four-year-old looked over at me and stuck her head in my side. I grabbed them both and said, "Everything's going to be all right." They were snotting up my clothes, and I didn't even care.

I asked them, "Your mom and dad are not together anymore?"

"No," they both said very sadly.

"You want them together, don't you?"

They shook their heads, "Yeah. "

I asked them if they knew Jesus. The nine-year-old said, "We go to Sunday school when we visit my Daddy."

I said, "Well, you know, Jesus knows what it is to be separated from His family too. He was separated from His Father for a while. He had to leave His Father, like you had to leave your father. He knows what you feel like, and He loves you.

"I know it hurts, so the next time you feel those pains, ask Jesus to help you. Sometimes mommies and daddies make mistakes, but Jesus will never leave you." I held them both and prayed for them.

When I finished, I looked up and the stewardess had stopped, and about six rows back everyone was crying.

When the plane landed, I walked out with the kids and met their mother. I talked to her about what had happened, and I said, "Sometimes we forget how much children can hurt. I know it's not easy being a single parent. You may have some hard times in your life, but Jesus can help you and your kids."

It was a real blessing for me to minister to that family. Faith gave me the ability to sing in the midst of two little girls' difficult and devastating circumstance.

An unseen audience listened. I was totally involved in the pains of the two little girls, yet people six rows back were listening, and their hearts were touched by the love of Jesus.

As I told the girls about Jesus and His love for them, it chased the gloom away. As the light began to shine in the plane, I didn't have to argue with anyone. People were moved by the Holy Spirit.

You too can be a light in a dark place. Let your light shine and sing a song in the night. You don't have to try to change anyone, just let the light of God bring the ministry of cheerfulness into their life.

Cheerfulness is infectious. Pass it on!

Jesse Duplantis is a dynamic evangelist called to minister God's message of salvation through Jesus Christ to the world. From New Orleans, Louisiana, Jesse is anointed by God with a unique preaching ministry that melts even the hardest heart with hilarious illustrations and strong biblical teaching.

Since 1978, Jesse's primary goal has been to spread the Gospel. He has become a popular guest speaker at church meetings, conventions, seminars, Bible colleges, and on Christian television programs across America. His anointed sermons point sinners to Calvary and motivate Christians to exercise their authority over the devil by realizing their position in Christ.

Jesse believes that Christianity is not just something you talk about on Sunday; it is a day-to-day fellowship with the Lord Jesus Christ. It is this close fellowship with Jesus that makes the impossible suddenly possible.

Jesse's weekly thirty minute television program has touched millions of lives with the Gospel of Jesus. His program can be seen on over 2,700 television stations across the globe.

Through anointed biblical preaching, Jesse is bringing God's message of hope to our generation. A message that cuts through all denominational barriers, transcends human hyprocrisy and frailty, and reaches the heart of mankind.

Look for these other books by
Jesse Duplantis

New! The Everyday Visionary

Wanting a God You Can Talk To
Also available in Braille

What in Hell Do You Want?

Jambalaya for the Soul
Also available in Braille

Breaking the Power of Natural Law
Also available in Braille

God Is Not Enough, He's Too Much!
Also available in Braille

Heaven: Close Encounters of the God Kind
Also available in Braille and Spanish

Jesse's Mini-Books

Don't Be Affected by the World's Message
The Battle of Life
Running Toward Your Giant
Keep Your Foot on the Devil's Neck
One More Night With the Frogs
Leave it in the Hands of a Specialist
The Sovereignty of God
Understanding Salvation
Also available in Spanish

JESSE DUPLANTIS MINISTRIES
"Preaching the Gospel to the World"